34880000823224

BOOK CHARGING CARD

Call No. WIN

Accession No. _____

Author Winans, Jay D.

Title Delaware

Borrower's Name	Date Returned

975.1
WIN

Winans, Jay D.
Delaware
34880000 823224

DELAWARE

Jay D. Winans

Published by Weigl Publishers Inc.
123 South Broad Street, Box 227
Mankato, MN   56002
USA
Web site: http://www.weigl.com

Library of Congress Cataloging-in-Publication Data available upon request from the publisher. Fax: (507) 388-2746 for the attention of the Publishing Records Department.

ISBN 1-930954-99-9

Printed in the United States of America
1 2 3 4 5 6 7 8 9 10   05 04 03 02 01

Editor
Michael Lowry
Copy Editor
Heather Kissock
Designers
Warren Clark
Terry Paulhus
Photo Researcher
Gayle Murdoff

Photograph Credits

Every reasonable effort has been made to trace ownership and to obtain permission to reprint copyright material. The publishers would be pleased to have any errors or omissions brought to their attention so that they may be corrected in subsequent printings.

Cover: Drummer Boy (Delaware Tourism Office), Holly (Corel Corporation); **The Academy of the Dance:** page 25T; **The Atwater Kent Museum:** page 16B; **Corbis Corporation:** page 14T; **Corel Corporation:** pages 5BL, 8T, 9T, 11T, 15T, 14BL, 28T, 28B, 29T, 29B; **Delaware Public Archives:** pages 18B, 19; **Delaware Tourism Office:** pages 3T, 3M, 4T, 4B, 5T, 6T, 6B, 7B, 8B, 9B, 10T, 10B, 11BL, 11BR, 12T, 12BL, 12BR, 13B, 15B, 17B, 18T, 21T, 21B, 22B, 23T, 25B, 25BL, 26T, 26B, 27T, 27B; **DuPont:** page 13T; **Eyewire Corporation:** pages 7T, 14B; **Kevin Fleming/Corbis:** pages 3B, 20T, 20B, 23B; **Minnesota Historical Society/Corbis:** page 24T; **Mosaic Images/Corbis:** page 24B; **National Archives of Canada C-17727:** page 17T; **Joseph Sohm; Chromosohm Inc./Corbis:** page 22T; **Marilyn "Angel" Wynn:** page 16T.

CONTENTS

INTRODUCTION

Delaware's first Swedish settlers arrived aboard the *Kalmar Nyckel* in 1638. A replica of the ship is on display at Fort Christina State Park.

Located on the Eastern Seaboard, Delaware has the unique honor of being the first state to **ratify** the United States Constitution, giving the state the nickname "The First State." Two Delawarians, John Dickinson and George Read, helped draft the constitution, which was **unanimously** approved by the state on December 7, 1787—a full five days before any other state.

While exploring the coastline north of Virginia in 1610, Captain Samuel Argall found refuge during a storm in a bay that he named in honor of the governor at Jamestown—Sir Thomas West, Baron de la Warr, or Delaware. Eventually, not only the bay but the river that flowed into the bay, the entire coastal area, and even the Native peoples who lived there came to be known as Delaware.

Residents in Georgetown celebrate a unique tradition called "Return Day." After elections, voters "return" to the city square where election results are read by the Town Crier.

QUICK FACTS

Delaware's flag depicts the state coat of arms in the center of a diamond upon a field of colonial blue.

Thomas Jefferson declared Delaware a "jewel" among the states, which is why one of its nicknames is "The Diamond State."

Delaware is also known as "The Blue Hen State," "The Peach State," and "Small Wonder."

The capital of Delaware is Dover.

Amtrak services
Wilmington with
fifty-five trains per day.

Getting There

Delaware lies on the Delmarva Peninsula, which it shares
with Maryland. Delaware borders Pennsylvania to the north,
and Maryland to the south and west. New Jersey is across
the Delaware Bay and the Delaware River is at the
northwest tip of the state. The state's eastern boundary
is the Atlantic Ocean.

The Delaware Memorial Bridge crosses the Delaware River
and connects northern Delaware with New Jersey. Southern
Delaware is linked to New Jersey by the Cape May-Lewes
Ferry, which crosses the
Delaware Bay. Major
highways, including the
I-95, I-295, and the New
Jersey Turnpike, travel
through the most populated
section of the state—the
city of Wilmington and its
surrounding area in the
extreme north. Wilmington
is a short drive from
numerous major cities,
including Philadelphia,
Baltimore, New York,
and Washington, D.C.

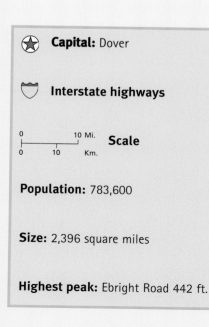

Capital: Dover

Interstate highways

Scale
0 — 10 Mi.
0 — 10 Km.

Population: 783,600

Size: 2,396 square miles

Highest peak: Ebright Road 442 ft.

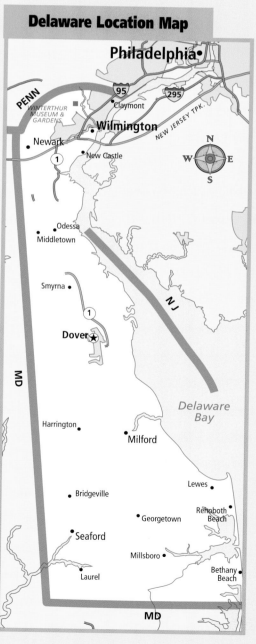

Delaware Location Map

During the American Civil War, Delaware fought for the Union.

QUICK FACTS

Nearly half of the men from Delaware who participated in the Battle of Antietam during the American Civil War died.

Delaware's state motto is "Liberty and Independence."

Delaware was ruled by several different countries before it became a state. In 1638, Sweden established a permanent colony at Fort Christina, in the same location as present-day Wilmington. New Sweden prospered and found a lasting peace with the local Native Peoples, but the colony failed to grow because it was unsupported by Sweden. Eventually, New Sweden was taken over by the Dutch in 1655 and renamed New Netherland. The Dutch, in turn, were conquered by the English in 1664, and the three counties of Delaware became part of the land given to William Penn, founder of Pennsylvania, in 1682. Delaware was governed from Philadelphia, Pennsylvania, until the American Revolution.

In 1776, Delaware cast the deciding vote for the Declaration of Independence. On July 1, Caesar Rodney rode 80 miles through a thunderstorm in the middle of the night from Wilmington to Independence Hall in Philadelphia. Rodney arrived at the hall still wearing his spurs and voted in favor of independence from British rule.

The Delaware Breakwater Lighthouse in Lewes Harbor was first lit in 1885.

QUICK FACTS

Many of the companies that are headquartered in Delaware do the majority of their business outside the state.

The official state mineral is sillimanite.

Henry Heimlich, a surgeon and inventor, was born in Wilmington. He developed the "Heimlich maneuver," which is used to save people from choking to death.

Delaware's state song is "Our Delaware" by George Hynson and William Brown.

Colonial blue and buff are the official state colors. The colors represent those of General George Washington's uniform.

The vast majority of Delaware's population lives in and around industrial Wilmington.

The small size of the state has made it necessary for companies in Delaware to do business with partners in other states. Pennsylvania, Maryland, New Jersey, and New York are all important business partners for Delaware. Today, Wilmington is just one of a group of cities that form an industrial and densely populated region, which stretches from Baltimore, Maryland, to Boston, Massachusetts. These cities are an important part of the national economy.

Delaware's business laws make the state attractive to companies throughout the United States. It is easier and cheaper to form a company in Delaware than it is in most other states. As a result, there are more company headquarters in Delaware than in any other state. Delaware's relaxed business laws have proven to be a major source of revenue for the state.

More than half of all Fortune 500 companies are from Delaware. The Fortune 500 is an annual list of the top 500 companies in the country.

Wilmington is Delaware's largest city. It was originally named "Willingtown," after one of its founders, Thomas Willing.

The Delaware River is one of the longest rivers without a dam in the eastern United States.

LAND AND CLIMATE

Delaware has the second lowest **elevation** in the country—only Florida has a lower elevation. The state can be divided into two main regions—the Coastal Plain and the Piedmont Plateau. The coast is marshy with numerous **tributary** streams and rivers flowing to the ocean. The southern portion of the state is sandy, but more fertile soil can be found inland throughout the majority of the state. The state's elevation increases in the northern Piedmont region, which extends south from Pennsylvania.

Delaware's climate is similar to other middle Atlantic states. The summers are hot and humid, with an average July temperature of 75° Fahrenheit. Winters in the state are cool, and average temperatures are a mild 35°F. The average yearly precipitation in Delaware is 45 inches.

QUICK FACTS

In 1889, a huge storm off the coast of Delaware destroyed forty ships and killed seventy people.

The Christina River is a tributary of the Delaware River, and the Brandywine River is a tributary of the Christina River.

The town of Delmar is located in both Delaware and Maryland. The **Mason-Dixon line** passes through the town.

The average elevation in Delaware is approximately 60 feet. Ebright Road is the highest point in the state at only 442 feet, while the lowest point is sea level at the Atlantic coastline.

The Mason-Dixon Monument, near Delmar, marks the beginning of the Mason-Dixon line.

Delaware produces about 84 million pounds of watermelons every year.

NATURAL RESOURCES

Natural resources in Delaware are not numerous and make up only a small part of the state's economy. The state sits on a foundation of gravel and sand, and offers very little in the way of mineral resources for mining operations. In fact, Delaware ranks last in the nation in the value of mineral production, earning about $10 million a year. All three counties in Delaware produce sand and gravel. The state is also a source for Brandywine blue granite, a building stone used for decoration.

The level landscape, moderate coastal climate, and reasonably fertile soil provide Delaware farmers with the means to raise crops. The money earned from crops accounts for about 20 percent of the state's farm income. Soybeans and corn are the two most valuable crops. Barley, peas, potatoes, and wheat are also grown in the state.

QUICK FACTS

In 1930, the **peat** in the Pocomoke Swamp burned for 8 months due to a disastrous fire.

Belemnite is the official state fossil.

Lewes is home to a plant that processes seawater to produce magnesium. Magnesium is Delaware's leading mineral product.

Delaware's 2,400 farms cover nearly 50 percent of the state.

Round white potatoes are the most common type of potato grown in Delaware.

The peach blossom was named the official state flower in 1895.

PLANTS AND ANIMALS

One third of Delaware is covered by forests. Common trees in the state include beech, hickory, holly, oak, and sweet gum. Wildflowers flourish in the state's swamps and marshes. The Cypress Swamp that straddles the Delaware and Maryland border in the south is the most northern location of the bald cypress. Azaleas, magnolias, pink and white hibiscus, and violets are a colorful part of the state's landscape.

Delaware's Atlantic shore attracts seabirds and other coastal wildlife to the salt marshes. Further inland, round ponds called Carolina bays are the only places where certain rare species of plants survive. Delaware has 132,000 acres of freshwater wetlands and almost 90,000 acres of tidal wetlands. These areas are a crucial habitat for Delaware's coastal wildlife. In 1963, the state government established the Prime Hook National Wildlife Refuge to protect the wildlife of the wetlands.

Farmers near the Prime Hook Wildlife Refuge leave a portion of their crops in the field to provide food for waterfowl and other wildlife.

Delaware's animal population can be found in fields, rivers, and forests throughout the state. Beaver, deer, fox, mink, muskrat, otter, rabbit, and raccoon all live in Delaware.

Birding is a popular pastime in Delaware because of the abundance and variety of birds. There are 380 species of birds from 45 different families in the state. The wetlands of Delaware Bay attract huge numbers of migrating waterfowl to the western shore. More than 100,000 snow geese, Canada geese, and other migrating birds spend the winter months in Delaware. Black-bellied plovers, ruddy turnstones, red knots, and sandpipers can be seen in May searching for horseshoe crabs' eggs along the bay's shoreline.

Canadian geese use star patterns, landmarks on the earth, and distinctive smells when migrating every spring and fall.

The state's lakes and ponds contain a variety of fish, including bass, carp, eel, and trout. Delaware's coastal waters are home to clams, crabs, oysters, and sea trout.

QUICK FACTS

Delaware's state fish is the weakfish, also known as the sea trout, gray trout, yellow mouth, yellow fin trout, squeteague, or tiderunner.

The blue hen chicken is the state bird of Delaware.

The official state bug is the ladybug.

Despite the abundance of birds and other wildlife in Delaware, fifteen animal species are on the federal list of endangered species, including five species of turtles.

In May, Delaware beaches are covered in horseshoe crabs, which emerge from the ocean to lay their eggs in the sand.

Ladybugs have a large appetite for garden aphids. A single ladybug may consume as many as 5,000 aphids in its lifetime.

Rehoboth is the nation's largest coastal resort town.

TOURISM

Delaware's beaches are the most popular tourist and outdoor destinations in the state, drawing 6 million visitors per year. Nearly 25 miles of sandy Atlantic beaches extend from the tip of Delaware Bay to the Maryland border. Half of these are located in state parks.

The Historic Houses of Odessa, in New Castle county, provide visitors with an insight into life in the eighteenth and nineteenth centuries. Strolling down the quiet streets, tourists can visit the Corbit-Sharp House, which is listed on the National Register of Historic Places. The house contains examples of beautiful furniture made by local cabinetmakers.

One last stop in Delaware should be the Johnson-Victrola Museum. The museum is a tribute to Eldridge Reeves Johnson, from Wilmington. Johnson helped invent the **gramophone** and founded the Victor Talking Machine Company, which later became RCA Victor. Johnson also improved the quality of vinyl records by applying electric currents to wax.

The Johnson-Victrola Museum, in Dover, contains dozens of examples of early "talking machines."

The DuPont research center, near Wilmington, is one of the largest chemical science research facilities in the world.

QUICK FACTS

Delaware's economy is based mainly on manufacturing.

The DuPont name is well-known not only for the products it manufactures and the large work force it employs, but also for the numerous family members who have served as politicians and community leaders in Delaware.

The first DuPont factory has been transformed into the Hagley Museum. The large outdoor museum celebrates the origins of the company.

Seaford was once known as "The Nylon Capital of the World" because that was where DuPont first manufactured the material.

INDUSTRY

At the beginning of the nineteenth century, Eleuthère Irénée du Pont de Nemours, a Frenchman who emigrated to Delaware as a refugee of the French Revolution, began operating a gunpowder factory on a property near the Brandywine River. Soon, the factory was producing enough powder to supply the United States government during its involvement in the War of 1812, the Mexican War, the American Civil War, and vast building projects, such as the transcontinental railroad and the Panama Canal. In the twentieth century, DuPont developed its business beyond the manufacturing of gunpowder and began to produce materials, such as nylon, that were based on modern chemistry. Today, DuPont is the largest manufacturer of science-based goods in the United States.

Delaware is also home to other manufacturing and processing industries. These include automobile-assembly plants, oil refineries, packaging plants, textile mills, and food-processing plants.

The Chrysler car-manufacturing plant is one of Delaware's major employers.

GOODS AND SERVICES

The sale of goods is another important part of Delaware's economy. In the state's earliest days, the sale of agricultural products provided the majority of the state's income. In the 1700s, Delaware's flour mills were renowned. In fact, the price for wheat was set in Wilmington. Paper and cotton mills were established in Brandywine Village toward the end of the eighteenth century. As the **Industrial Revolution** gave rise to automation, factories began to play a greater role in Delaware's economy.

Companies such as DuPont, Hercules, and ICI Americas are responsible for producing a majority of the chemicals, dyes, and powders that make Delaware "The Chemical Capital of the World." These companies produce pigments, petrochemicals, rubber, nylon, and plastics that are used all over the world.

Nylon is an extremely durable material that is used in everything from backpacks to toothbrushes. Nylon was invented in Delaware.

QUICK FACTS

In 1785, Oliver Evans built the first completely automatic flour mill in the country. He built the mill on Red Clay Creek, near his hometown of Newport.

Wallace Carouthers invented the synthetic fiber known as nylon in 1935 while he was employed at DuPont.

During the nineteenth century, building railroad cars was a major industry in Delaware.

Many credit card companies have operations in Wilmington.

Delaware is considered one of the nation's leaders in scientific research and management.

The average weight of a Delaware broiler chicken is 5.9 pounds.

Since the early part of the twentieth century, Delaware has maintained very liberal **incorporation** laws. These laws encouraged businesses to establish their headquarters in Delaware. In the 1980s, large banks began to move to Delaware to take advantage of the reduced taxes on financial institutions.

Livestock products are an important part of Delaware's economy. The **broiler-chicken** business accounts for more than 70 percent of Delaware's farm income and is one of the state's largest enterprises. Yearly sales of broiler chickens earn the state more than $490 million. Sussex County, the number one broiler-chicken producing county in the United States, is home to approximately 600 million chickens—766 times the human population of the county. The majority of the grain grown in Delaware is used to feed chickens.

QUICK FACTS

Fisher's Popcorn, a company on Fenwick Island, makes internationally renowned caramel corn.

There is no sales tax in the state of Delaware.

Delaware's fishers harvest clams, crabs, oysters, and some fish.

The annual catch of Delaware's fishing industry is worth about $8 million.

FIRST NATIONS

Chief La-pa-win-so, leader of the Lenni Lenape, was one of the key figures responsible for signing the Walking Purchase Treaty.

QUICK FACTS

The Lenni Lenape play a traditional game called Pahsahëmen, similar to football, in which the men play against the women. The men are only permitted to kick the ball, while the women may throw and carry the ball as well.

Between 1600 and 1900, the Lenni Lenape were forced to relocate more than twenty times.

The Nanticoke, who were related to the Lenni Lenape, once controlled most of the Delmarva Peninsula.

The Lenni Lenape fought British expansion in the French and Indian War, and for a time, even supported the American Revolution.

When the Europeans first arrived, they met the area's Native Peoples, who the Europeans named the Delaware. The Delaware actually called themselves the *Lenni Lenape*, which means "original people." Part of the Algonquian-language group, they lived along the Atlantic Seaboard from the area of Cape Henlopen in Delaware, to Long Island in New York.

At first, the Lenni Lenape enjoyed a friendly relationship with the Europeans. In 1737, in an event that came to be known as the Walking Purchase, William Penn falsely claimed that the Lenni Lenape's ancestors had sold land to the Penns more than 50 years before. According to a false **deed**, all the land within one-and-a-half-days' walk was to be given to the Penns. The Penns then measured the area using three of their best runners, thus acquiring 1,200 square miles of land. The Lenape complained but ultimately accommodated the Penns and moved off the land.

In the past, ornaments of bone, shell, and wampum were sometimes worn by Lenni Lenape women as necklaces, or on wrists and ankles.

Henry Hudson is thought to be one of the first European explorers to anchor in Delaware Bay.

EXPLORERS AND MISSIONARIES

Delaware's shores were first spotted by Henry Hudson in 1609. Hudson was an English explorer employed by the Dutch. At the time, Hudson was in search of the Northwest Passage, a waterway that was rumored to connect the Atlantic and Pacific Oceans. On his way to exploring the area around New York Harbor and the Hudson River, Hudson sailed into Delaware Bay and past the mouth of the Delaware River.

In 1610, Captain Samuel Argall named the Delaware Bay while exploring the coast north of Virginia. Other notable explorers of Delaware's coastal waters were Cornelius May in 1613, and Cornelius Hendricksen in 1614. Hendricksen traveled up the Delaware River and traded with the Native Peoples.

QUICK FACTS

Some scientists have suggested that the lotus plants found in Delaware may be evidence of Egyptian excursions to the North American coastline in ancient times.

Augustine Hermann, the man who mapped the Delmarva Peninsula in the mid-1600s, gave his name to Augustine Beach.

The Finns introduced the European-style log cabin to the United States. Finnish and Swedish settlers arrived in Delaware in the mid-1660s.

Dutch navigator Cornelius May was the first person to discover Fenwick Island.

The first log cabin in Delaware was built with a crawl space between the floor and earth. It was used as sleeping quarters for children and as storage space.

The Zwaanandael Museum, in Lewes, contains exhibits that illustrate the history of Delaware's first Dutch settlement.

EARLY SETTLERS

The first European settlers arrived in the Delaware area in 1631, only 11 years after the pilgrims landed at Plymouth. These first settlers were Dutchmen who were members of a trading company formed by David Pietersen de Vries. Thirty settlers sailed from Hoorn, Netherlands, in the ship *De Walis* under the command of Captain Peter Heyes. When they arrived in North America they founded a settlement near what is now Lewes and Rehoboth Canal. They named the settlement *Zwaanendael*, which means "the valley of the swans."

In 1632, de Vries set sail for a visit to the colony. When he arrived, he found the camp destroyed and the bones of the company members lying in the fields. He was told by the Native Peoples who lived nearby that there had been a battle between the *Zwaanendael* settlers and the Native Peoples. None of the Dutchmen had survived the conflict. The reason for the battle was a series of misunderstandings between the settlers and the Native Americans.

QUICK FACTS

In 1613, Captain Samuel Argall kidnapped Pocahontas, daughter of Chief Powhatan. Argall held her as a hostage to be exchanged for English prisoners held by her father.

In 1635, George Holmes, an Englishman from a colony in Connecticut, Thomas Hall, and a dozen others tried to move to the Delaware River area, but they were captured and taken prisoner by the Dutch who claimed the area.

New Sweden was the only colony ever established by the Swedish in North America. At the height of its prosperity, New Sweden's population numbered about 350 people.

QUICK FACTS

In 1655, David Pietersen de Vries wrote the *Korte Historiael*, which provided a history of New Netherland.

Peter Minuit helped found New Amsterdam, which later became New York City.

In the 1600s, the *Kalmar Nyckel* made four round trips across the Atlantic Ocean, which is more than any other colonial ship during that same time.

The Kalmar Nyckel brought twenty-four Swedish, Finnish, Dutch, and German settlers to the New World. The twenty-fifth settler, named Anthoni, was a **freedman** from the Caribbean.

In 1638, Peter Minuit, a Dutchman and the former governor of New Amsterdam, led a group of Swedish colonists to the area that has become Wilmington. They arrived in the ships *Kalmar Nyckel* and *Vogel Grip* and landed on the shores of the Christina River. Here, they established a settlement at Fort Christina, named in honor of Sweden's young queen. New Sweden prospered under the able leadership of Colonel Johan Printz, who ruled the new colony from 1643 until 1653. Despite his repeated requests for supplies and other resources, Sweden failed to provide for the colony. In 1653, Printz finally left in anger over Sweden's failure to support the new colony. Ironically, Queen Christina sent a boatload of supplies and approximately 300 colonists to New Sweden just as Printz was leaving.

In 1654, Johan Rising, the new governor, captured Fort Casmir, the Dutch fortification on the north bank of the Delaware River. He was not able to keep the fort for long, as Peter Stuyvesant, the governor of New Amsterdam, recaptured the fort and all of New Sweden in 1655, bringing an end to Swedish colonies in the New World.

Between 1638 and 1656, Swedish colonists made twelve expeditions to the New World. The first expedition founded a colony in Delaware.

POPULATION

Almost 25 percent of Delaware's population is under the age of 18.

Delaware is one of the most densely populated states in the country. A large percentage of the 783,600 people live in the urban and industrial centers in the northern portion of the state. The average **population density** in the state is 400 people per square mile.

About 74 percent of Delaware's population are of European descent, another 19 percent are African American, 4.7 percent are Hispanic or Latin American, 2 percent are Asian American, and 0.3 percent are Native American.

In the 1990s, Delaware experienced higher than average population growth compared to the rest of the United States. The population of Delaware grew by 17.6 percent, whereas the national population grew by 13 percent.

QUICK FACTS

Homeownership in Delaware is more common than in the rest of the country. Only 66 percent of the nation's citizens own their own homes, but Delaware's ownership rate is at 72 percent.

Delaware's households also have a higher average yearly income—$41,300— than the rest of the country—$37,000.

About 27 percent of Delaware's population lives outside of cities.

The Legislative Hall is located in Dover, the state's capital.

POLITICS AND GOVERNMENT

Though the state of Delaware was the first to ratify the United States Constitution, it did not adopt a state constitution until 1897. According to the state constitution, the governor serves as head of the executive branch of Delaware, serving a four-year term, and may be re-elected only once. Other members of the executive branch include the lieutenant governor, attorney general, insurance commissioner, and treasurer.

The General Assembly, or legislature, heads the legislative branch. The legislature is composed of twenty-one senators and forty-one members of the House of Representatives.

All Delaware judges are appointed by the governor. The state's judicial branch is made up of three courts—a supreme court, a superior court, and a court of chancery. There are also local courts found throughout the state's three counties.

Delaware's motto was added to the state seal in 1847.

The Georgetown Hispanic festival is a celebration of Hispanic culture and food.

CULTURAL GROUPS

As founders of one of the first settlements in Delaware, the Swedish have left a rich heritage in the state. The Holy Trinity Church, or Old Swedes, is the nation's oldest standing church still in operation. The church was built in Wilmington in 1698 by descendants of the first Swedish settlers. Each December, the church celebrates the traditional Swedish Festival of Light in honor of Sankta Lucia. Sankta Lucia, an important figure in Swedish tradition, carries the message of Christmas, coming with light in her hair on the darkest morning of the year. She is a symbol of compassion, love, and light.

Delaware's African-American population grew in the mid-1900s as African Americans migrated from the South to the industrialized north. More than 10,000 people turn out each year for "Positively Dover," an African-American festival that celebrates the state's rich African-American heritage.

Participants in Dover's annual African-American Festival wear traditional African clothing to celebrate their culture.

A small community of Native Americans is found in Cheswold, Kent County. The 500 remaining Nanticokes originated in the Maryland region. In 1979, the Nanticoke held their first powwow since the 1940s. Today, the Nanticoke Indian Pow Wow is among the largest traditional powwows on the east coast. This celebration of dance and culture attracts visitors from across the country.

Amish farms and settlements dot the landscape around the outskirts of Dover in Kent County. The Amish are members of a traditional farming society that avoids contact with the modern world. Amish beliefs restrict the use of modern technology, including the automobile and electricity. The Amish make all their own clothing, including colorful Amish quilts, which can be bought at roadside stands.

The name Nanticoke means "people of the tidewater."

QUICK FACTS

Little Italy, in Wilmington, is home to St. Anthony's annual Italian Festival, which takes place in June.

During the American Revolution, the Nanticokes fought on the side of the British.

The Nanticoke Indian Museum, in Millsboro, opened in 1984. It is the only Native-American museum in Delaware and contains exhibits that are more than 10,000 years old.

The horse and buggy is one of the major methods of transportation among the Amish.

After they marry, Amish men begin to grow out their beards. A long beard is a sign of adulthood.

Even though Clifford Brown died when he was only 25 years old, his influence on the world of jazz is still felt today.

ARTS AND ENTERTAINMENT

Delaware's most important contribution to the history of art is the work of Howard Pyle. Born in 1853 in Wilmington, Pyle is known for the realism and the historical detail of his illustrations. Hailed as the founder of modern American illustration, Pyle taught and influenced countless young illustrators, including Maxfield Parrish and N.C. Wyeth. These pupils changed the world of illustration and are known as "The Brandywine School," after the school that Pyle founded in Wilmington in 1900.

Felix Darley was another great illustrator of the nineteenth century. He spent the last 29 years of his life in Claymount, where he produced many of his best-known illustrations. Darley's fame and popularity arose from his illustrations for the novels of great writers such as Charles Dickens, Nathaniel Hawthorne, and Edgar Allan Poe.

Howard Pyle's illustration, *The Battle of Nashville,* was created in 1906.

The Delaware Art Museum was started by a group of Wilmington **patrons** who wished to put forty-eight of Howard Pyle's artworks on display. Since that time, the museum has built a permanent collection of American illustrations, with a special emphasis on Pyle's work. The collection also includes works by Edward Hopper, Frederic Edwin Church, Deborah Butterfield, and John Sloan, as well as the most important collection of English **Pre-Raphaelite** art in the United States.

The Wilmington Ballet Company is Delaware's oldest professional ballet company. The company provides performance and training experience for dancers and gives community performances featuring internationally known dancers.

OPERADELAWARE is Wilmington's opera company. OPERADELAWARE performances are held at the Grand Opera House and are accompanied by a live orchestra. The company performs world premieres and family operas, as well as educational, community, and regional outreach programs.

The Wilmington Ballet Company was founded in 1981 in Wilmington.

QUICK FACTS

Television actress Valerie Bertinelli was born in Wilmington.

OPERADELAWARE is one of the oldest opera companies in the country. It has been staging performances for more than 57 years.

The Delaware Art Museum was founded in 1912.

The Pre-Raphaelite painters produced detailed and highly realistic works of art based on medieval and biblical history.

Delaware's sports fans often turn out to support the University of Delaware's Fightin' Blue Hens.

SPORTS

A small state such as Delaware does not have a large enough population to attract a professional sports team. Instead, Delaware's enthusiastic sports fans have the opportunity to enjoy a large variety of community and college level sports. The Wilmington Blue Rocks play single "A" baseball at Frawley Stadium. The team is **affiliated** with the Kansas City Royals, a Major League Baseball team. Another popular team is the Delaware Bobcats, a women's ice hockey team. The Bobcats have been playing since 1975.

Delaware fans also follow the success of the Fightin' Blue Hens of the University of Delaware at Newark. The university's sports program includes baseball, men's and women's basketball, football, field hockey, golf, men's and women's lacrosse, men's and women's soccer, volleyball, men's and women's tennis, softball, women's rowing, and a variety of track and swimming teams.

The University of Delaware's football team is named after the official state bird, the blue hen.

Delaware's professional women's golf association is the country's oldest women's sports association. It was established in 1950.

QUICK FACTS

The Delaware Smash represents Delaware in World Team Tennis, which is the only **unisex** team sport in the United States.

Delaware Sports is a half-hour television show that has been providing high-school and college-sports coverage since 1995.

Golf is another favored form of recreation in Delaware. Baywood Greens is an 18-hole championship golf course located in Long Neck. Baywood features 8 timbered bridges, 27 acres of ponds, 2 tunnels, and more than 200,000 flowers, shrubs, and trees.

Sport fishing is also hugely popular in Delaware. Each year, a weakfish contest is sponsored, which includes prizes for the largest weakfish caught. Another popular contest is the Delaware Sport Fishing Tournament, which lasts throughout the year. Contestants compete in a variety of freshwater and saltwater categories, including bluefish, marlin, swordfish, and trout.

Hiking is a fantastic and inexpensive way to enjoy Delaware's great outdoors. The state has more than 80 miles of trails that wind through ten state parks. Avid hikers can take the Trail Challenge, which involves hiking fifteen state-park trails within a period of one year. Winners of the Trail Challenge receive the Golden Boot Award.

The Wilmington Blue Rocks have the second-best winning percentage in all of Minor League Baseball.

Brain Teasers

1

True or False:

Delaware is the only state without a national park system.

Answer: True. Delaware has no national parks, seashores, battlefields, memorials, or monuments.

2

Settlers from which country landed at "The Rocks"?

a) Sweden

b) Finland

c) Norway

d) Denmark

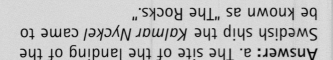

Answer: a. The site of the landing of the Swedish ship the *Kalmar Nyckel* came to be known as "The Rocks."

3

Delaware's state seal depicts a sheaf of wheat, an ear of corn, and what?

a) a weakfish

b) a ladybug

c) a peach tree

d) an ox

Answer: d. The ox is a symbol of the importance of livestock to the state's early economy.

4

True or False:

The smallest county in Delaware contains the largest population.

Answer: True. More than 500,000 people live in New Castle County in the north, which is about 64 percent of the state's entire population.

5

The United States battleship USS *Delaware* was **commissioned** in what year?

a) 1710

b) 1810

c) 1910

d) 2001

Answer: c. The USS *Delaware* was commissioned in 1910.

6

True or False:

Delaware was used as a lookout post for German U-boats during World War II.

Answer: *True.* Twelve concrete observation towers were built along the coast of Delaware.

7

Delaware's highest sand dune is how tall?

a) 20 feet

b) 80 feet

c) 150 feet

d) 420 feet

Answer: b. The Great Dune at Cape Henlopen State Park in Lewes is 80 feet tall.

8

Who was known as the "Penman of the Revolution"?

Answer: John Dickinson, from Dover, earned the nickname for his many political writings during the American Revolution.

FOR MORE INFORMATION

Books

Adams, Charles J. and David J. Seibold. *Shipwrecks, Sea Stories and Legends of the Delaware Coast*. Reading, PA: Exeter House Books, 1989.

Dale, Frank. *Delaware Diary: Episodes in the Life of a River*. Piscataway, NJ: Rutgers University Press, 1996.

Milford, Phil. *Delaware Trivia*. Nashville: Rutledge Hill Press, 2001.

Weslager, Clinton A. *The Delaware Indians: A History*. Piscataway, NJ: Rutgers University Press, 1990.

Web Sites

You can also go online and have a look at the following Web sites:

Government of Delaware
http://www.delaware.gov/

50 States: Delaware
http://www.50states.com/delaware.htm

Delaware Toursim Office
http://www.visitdelaware.net/

Some Web sites stay current longer than others. To find other Delaware Web sites, enter search terms such as "Delaware," "The First State," "Dover," or any other topic you want to research.

GLOSSARY

affiliated: connected with

broiler chicken: a young chicken raised for meat rather than eggs

commissioned: brought into active service

deed: a sealed contract, usually relating to property

elevation: height above sea level

freedman: a person who has been freed from slavery

gramophone: an early record player

incorporation: the formation of a corporation or company

Industrial Revolution: the widespread replacement of manual labor by machines in the late-1700s, began in Great Britain and spread to the United States

Mason-Dixon line: a boundary between Pennsylvania and Maryland that served as a divider between free and slave states before the American Civil War; named after the British surveyors Charles Mason and Jeremiah Dixon

patrons: wealthy people who support the arts

peat: organic material found in damp and marshy regions, often cut and dried for use as a fuel

population density: the average number of people per unit of area

Pre-Raphaelite: a secret society of painters in the mid-1800s who were named after the sixteenth century Italian painter, Raphael

ratify: approve

tributary: a stream that flows into another stream or river

unanimously: agreed by everyone

unisex: for both male and female

INDEX